Erase to Create

'I' Just Want to be Happy!

Andrea Jóba LCH Dip.

British Library Cataloguing in Publication Data Act catalogue entry for this book is available from the British Library. Paperback edition.

ISBN 978-0-9576895-2-7

Thank you with love

"Andrea has put herself into these poems by cleverly combining her emotional self with her training in Ho'oponopono. The poems start with self-talk and all the rubbish she says to herself. Then she examines her need to be loved by this one special person, a thought provoking poem. There is a strong theme of suffering in the poems with fear, anger and rage coming through very powerfully. The poems move on to personal responsibility, Andrea incorporating her learning from the Life Coaching Diploma she attained. Throughout the poems Andrea draws out the fact that everyone needs to take personal responsibility for how we feel and what we choose to think, again giving her interpretation of her experience around the Ho'oponopono principles. The poems move onto the power of love to change life. Finally, Andrea moves into inspiration and how to move forward. You can take as much, or as little, as you want from these poems and you will be sure to re-visit them again and again as you transit on your life journey."

Curly Martin, International Bestselling Author, Director, Coach, Achievement Specialists Ltd

"Andrea bares her soul in this book of insightful poems. She shares with you her times of sadness and desolation, the journey that she has undertaken including forgiveness and letting go to a place of joy and love. I am sure that readers will sense the narrative of hope that Andrea is offering in many of her poems. This is a book that you can dip in, read, reflect and notice your own insights and learnings so you also can erase past despair and create a life of happiness, peace and love."

Lindsey Reed, International Coach, Trainer and Author – Glows Coaching

"This is a perfect book to dip into for inspiration, clarity and understanding of who you are. You can keep it by your bed and read it at the beginning and end of the day. It is ideal helping you to cope with life's challenge."

Helen Turier, Award winning author

"Andrea, I am pleased to hear about your success in applying Law of Attraction to the business community since your Certification in 2009. Your Certified Law of Attraction Facilitator is enhanced with your additional training and teaching you have incorporated to help businesses apply Law of Attraction for success. You have shown your commitment to this teaching by furthering your training tools and techniques. I would recommend any business to have you as their professional trainer. You are passionate about your work and that will serve your clients. Congratulations on your success."

Michael Losier – CEO Michael Losier Enterprises Inc.

I dedicate this book to 'I'

And to those who came and continue coming into my life to show me what I needed/need to erase in order to create a zero state of being.

Personal thanks to Lindsey Reed who is an inspiration, friend, who supported me on my journey and helped me to create this wonderful book.

I would like to thank the people who helped with my personal development and healing journey Maya, Mr Charles, Antonio, Pam Lidford, Curly Martin, Michael Losier, Phd. Ihaleakala Hew Len, Patrice and Danielle.

And the people who helped to give this book clarity, design and total transformation deserve a big thank you: Louise Lubke Cuss, Samantha Pearce and Richard Excell.

Author's Note

When I started to write this book, I wasn't aware of the powerful journey of self-discovery I was about to encounter and the transformations I would be going through. During my life I have experienced adversities that have led me to discover who I really am, what my problems are, where they are, how I can solve them and what my purpose of existence is. I wrote this book as I walked across a bridge to another new beginning of my life. If it will inspire, educate, transform, and give confidence and hope to others that is a bonus. When we take 100% responsibility for what is going on in us, we change the whole Cosmos. We can create clarity, happiness, balance, harmony and embrace our present moment. The more we fall in love with everything the more freedom we create and allow the path we have dreamt walking on beyond comprehension.

This book is about discovering the thoughts and stories I created within, how heavy I felt carrying them and how I was able to free myself from them and allow inspirations into my life. I felt that these poems can help others to reflect on their experiences or stories they created within their mind and will be able to give them confidence to allow their inspirations. In my experience, inspired results always seem to appear from the least expected source.

I started to write poems from a young age, especially when I was feeling hurt; that was my way of expressing my emotions. Since then I have learnt how I am able to express my emotions in a poem as well as confront and release them. I am happy and feel free by waving goodbye to pain, suffering and anger and leaving my burdens behind. I learnt to accept the love and beauty in me and hope to pass it on to others so they can also discover the same.

The Universe is in me and vice versa, therefore anything that appears in my existence I created. I have a choice to nurture the love in me and keep being in the flow or reject it. Both these options are open to me and it takes the same amount of time to focus on either one of them. I understand that it can be hard to make the first step towards transition; at one point in my life I was so depressed that I was scared to leave my home. My mind was embossed in grief, fear, guilt and sadness. It took me some time, but I chose to start a new life and slowly managed to rebuild my Universe. I am grateful for my past, because it taught me how to stay in the present: love moment by moment.

Contents

Chapter Zero: Love

Chapter Zero touches on who we are – the most precious being in the Universe. When we understand and recognise our core we are able to transfer that into every living entity including our business. When we love ourselves we are able to act from that frame of mind, which can only attract more of the same.

Just imagine when you were born, a beautiful, pure and infinite light and you started with a blank canvas. This was your natural state of mind. Now imagine that some dirt appears on this canvas, which you don't like, for example: your unwanted thoughts/emotions, anger, fear, stress or something else. You can leave this 'dirt' on the canvas and by doing so you will accumulate more of the same. Or you can choose to clear/delete this 'dirt' and return to your natural state of mind – beauty, pure and infinite light, which is the love that you are.

I understand that sometimes we crave love from others, because we can feel unloved and even fear that nobody will love us again.

We think the world is against us or that we are unlovable and many other fearful thoughts can enter our mind. These are the black marks on our white canvas and can send us into complete meltdown. Therefore it is our responsibility to eliminate these thoughts and go back to our natural state of mind and keep our canvas pristine.

At the end of this chapter you can reflect on what you discovered about who you are.

>*Love can eliminate any doubt and can create miracles in your life.*

>*As it is what you are, you can create your own Universe. Everything begins with you.*

Who Am I?

This poem is only for 'I',
What will 'I' discover and why?
Who am 'I' and what is my mission?
How can 'I' become a magician?

Do 'I' feel stuck or anxious each day?
Do 'I' give up or do 'I' run away?
Do 'I' see darkness and no chance?
Do 'I' have time to smile and dance?

How come everything is misty?
Why is my path rocky and twisty?
When 'I' arrived here on earth,
'I' was perfect and a lot of worth.

'I' looked in the mirror and 'I' see
The love 'I' 'lost' is really me.
By accepting this powerful device,
'I' am ready to play and roll the dice.

When 'I' am unsure which way to go,
'I' consider looking into my soul.
The key will be there, right within,
'I' reach for it and my freedom will begin.

Baby Ciara

When I looked into your eyes,
I saw the light and the blue skies.
You are the rainbow and the stars,
Your smile can be seen from Mars.

You show us how we should be,
In balance, and that we can be free.
You teach the world to be in joy,
Release our fears and pick up a toy.

The love that you are within,
It is all you need your life to begin.
Spread the kindness in your heart,
And admire your creative art.

May your life be blessed each day,
Whether you sleep, eat or play.
Thank you for your sparkling love,
Thank you for lifting me above.

Life

You are so beautiful and serene,
I knew you before you started to breathe,
I looked after you with my healing hands,
And the Divine in you understands.

Still innocent and without belief,
Your life started with ease.
Although sometimes you need to cry,
Your mother is there as an ally.

I wonder what will be your name.
Whether you will be there to claim?
I wonder if you were able to choose,
Would you be Summer, Spring or Blues?

As you breathe into your now
And getting to know how to allow.
You have a chance to make a fresh start,
Keep your family together, which is apart.

You have a chance to make amends,
Without doubt you will have many friends.
Keep your wonderful smile,
And your life will be worthwhile.

'Flower'

You bloom all year around,
Not many people notice your sound.
You are delicate and shy,
To whom special instructions apply.

You are transparent with a soft touch
And yet you are attached to your crutch.
Your natural way is to bloom and grow
And love yourself from top to toe.

You need much love and caring,
Looking after your roots and flaring.
Come rain or shine you need protecting,
Whether you are sleeping or blooming.

You are my favourite flower of all
And you are with me wherever I go.
You brighten my days with your smile
And I look after your gentle style.

Thank you for being in my 'park',
I am grateful for your spark.
This connection is for life,
I cherish every moment of the light.

Shaken Not Stirred

When you feel a heavy blow
And there is nowhere to go,
What you want is an easy exit,
But it is only you who can fix it.

What is it that you believe?
What is hiding under your sleeve?
What is it that you are afraid of?
Are you ready for the take off?

Abundance, confidence or camouflage,
Happiness, change or sabotage,
Decide the road you want to walk on,
And dedicate yourself to freedom.

My life flourished and got deeper,
I found my core, which felt steeper.
Balance and empowering belief,
And I said goodbye to my grief.

I love my thoughts that cried,
My life has turned a new tide.
I am finally being true to me,
And my choice is to be free.

The Light of 'I'

When I was born it was there
Like a soft and breezy air.
Shining in my heart and soul
Like the sun without control.

It goes beyond where eyes can see,
It is an endless growing tree.
It exists even if we are blind,
It lives in every human mind.

When I nurture my light within,
That is when love starts to begin.
I accept it in my heart and soul,
And I will fill every dark hole.

When I spread my light to others,
That is when I see my colours.
Gratitude is a value I care for,
It creates my abundance's core.

It shows me what love is truly,
It gives me joy and inner beauty.
It reflects the calming ocean,
It creates peace and devotion.

Accepting the light of 'I',
It is an easy tool to apply.
Freedom is the way to be,
I take the key that sets me free.

Chapter One: Thoughts

The thoughts and emotions I write about in this chapter were keeping me awake at night; I felt heavy, worried, stressed and hurt by the pain. We all have thoughts coming and going, that create our Universe and these thoughts come from within; I often say they are our most powerful enemies.

When I reacted from anger and frustration it always created negativity and most of all it didn't help me to erase my thoughts, quite the opposite: I attracted more of the same or worse. When I reacted from inspiration, for example happiness, I wasn't even aware as things just happened with ease.

I understand going through change or just realising that we have that bad thought can be hard, uncomfortable and even make us feel resentful.

Sometimes people fight tooth and nail against change, because they have been in their situation for so long that they feel comfortable in that environment.

In this chapter you might reflect and take an inventory of a thought that is making you feel uncomfortable, unhappy or you think is stopping you from achieving what you want in a particular area of your life.

I remember a particular incident in my life when we were thinking about extending our home so we could have more space. I was stuck with questioning the outcome and the process. Doubts, fears and other issues came up, then one day I stopped and literally looked at those emotions and I suddenly laughed. They were only illusions that I created in my mind. I simply asked myself: "So what do I want?" And I replied: "I just want to be happy!" There and then I released those toxic thoughts that contaminated my overall vibration. I would say within about an hour we heard good news, which helped us to raise the funds from a source least expected. My heart was brimming with abundance and love.

Fill your heart with the thought of love, beauty and peace.

What is the worst that can happen if you are already experiencing the worst? Give yourself a chance.

Soft – Soft Cuddles

When your life is full of muddle,
What you wish for is a cuddle.
When you wake up from a nightmare,
When you open your eyes and stare.

When you fall or when you are sad,
When everything is going bad.
When you feel the air is cold,
When there is no one to hold.

When you were a little boy,
And you couldn't find your toy.
When you were a little girl,
And you lost your shiny pearl.

When you heard the violent scream,
You wished you were by a stream.
When you saw the fights at night,
You wished you were in the light.

When others tortured your soul,
And you were under their control.
When you looked into the eyes of death,
When you felt you lost your breath.

When people rejected your heart,
It was very hard to depart.
When you heard that she is no more,
Your whole life fell to the floor.

I let my past dictate my present,
My guilt was as hard as cement.
I am ready to erase and let go,
Forgive and release my woe.

Thank you for your cuddles and love,
I know you are watching from above.
It is my time to be a hero,
Create clarity and be in 'zero'.

Blooms and Buds

Looking out to the inviting sunshine,
I am wondering: "Where is the sign?"
Where is that warming light?
What is wrong and what is right?

When things are not from the 'Source',
There can't be a real 'Life Force'.
The whole cosmos is in floods of tears,
And there won't be blossoms only fears.

I love you my dearest bud,
And I won't let you be stuck in a rut.
The water of life will nurture you,
Heal you when you feel blue.

You can only bloom and grow,
When the cleaning is in the flow,
It could be rain or shine,
Your abundant earth will align.

The Dirty Cloth

Stuck in this anger and pain,
Being tangled in the financial strain,
My body feels heavy and I can't move,
When will I get back my groove?

Why have you all left me behind?
What is making me blind?
I am washing the dirty cloth again,
But nothing appears in my brain.

'I' is sad and 'I' is blue,
She wants to put on the right shoe.
The anger and weight are inside,
Forgive and step away from the tide.

I am sorry for not loving you enough,
I am sorry that you had it so rough.
I am sorry for applying force,
I am sorry for doubting the 'Source'.

I neglected you for eons of time,
Please release me from this horrific crime.
I realise now that you are alive,
I will do everything for you to thrive.

I love you forever and will keep the flow,
I wrap you with the blanket of a rainbow.
I will cuddle you when you feel alone,
I will ease and heal your bemoan.

Release the anger and release the worry,
Release the need and release the hurry.
Release the fear of not having plenty,
Release the iron grip of the penny.

Trust the process and trust yourself,
Never doubt your Love's shelf.
And if your 'cloth' gets dirty again,
Just wash it and LOVE the stain.

Wish upon a Star

A little girl is staring at the sky,
Her wish is to see the world and fly.
The stars are shining above,
And all she wants is LOVE.

She lived through a lot of sorrow,
Which she didn't need to borrow,
She wants to break away from the 'prison',
And live her life in constant freedom.

Years went by and everything got harder,
Anger and fear filled up her larder.
And after 18 years of worry,
She packed her bags and left in a hurry.

She thought her wish was finally granted,
But she wasn't sure what she wanted.
More anger and worry appeared,
She was sad and really feared.

After 8 years her life was rocked,
She lost mind, body and soul in a shock.
Then slowly started to rebuild her 'I',
And she waved the past goodbye.

She remembered that little girl,
Who was longing for love with a pearl.
It was easier to blame others,
And she closed all the shutters.

As she was gazing at the stars again,
She knew her child was alone and in pain.
Then she saw a peaceful dove,
It said to her: "Forgive and Love."

Health

When you wonder about health,
What do you think it is worth?
What were you dealt at birth?
Was it strength or greedy wealth?

Can you accept the thought of cancer?
Can you believe a different answer?
Can you love and be able to let go?
Can you forgive your biggest foe?

Can you give up your toxic knots?
Can you erase your angry spots?
Are you willing to choose to change?
Embrace love and peace in exchange.

Are you stressed about making money?
Are you looking after your body?
Your health can bloom or forever shut,
You can transform or is there a 'but'?

When you want to end it all,
And inside your soul is a brawl.
Please see your unique light,
Keep going; it is worth the fight.

You are the Universal Love,
Stand up tall and rise above,
You have many options to choose,
Take the first step and you can't lose.

When your mind is free and open,
Your dreams cannot be broken.
It will create your perfect health
And transpire to your ideal wealth.

It is a unique gift to be alive,
I am grateful for my health and life.
The road forward is open and wide,
The wheel is within; 'I' choose the ride.

Pain

I am in pain and suffering,
My breathing is exhausting.
All my thoughts are disturbing
And I feel a volcano erupting.

I am in turmoil and madness,
What has taken over my happiness?
What is going on, I can't see,
Why is this happening to me?

Please dear 'child' help me to let go,
This heavy burden is blocking my soul.
I want to see the light and rainbow,
Feel the colours of blue, green and yellow.

The incredible rage and anger
It has been living here forever.
It controlled me for a long time,
This is a big mountain to climb.

Drowning in this whirlpool of fire,
I am trying to untangle this wire.
Oh my – it is so heavy and sad.
Please help me release all this bad.

These thoughts are cancerous
And 'mind suicide' is dangerous.
I can see now where the cord lies,
And slowly cut all the ties.

A gentle stream has started to flow,
I noticed a ray of hope with a glow.
This magnificent fire is now ceasing
And slowly love is increasing.

The eruption is gradually calming
And I can see flowers blossoming.
Lovely blue bonnets along the stream
And I sparkle in the sunbeam.

My shoulders are happy and lighter,
My mind is clean and brighter.
Thank you for releasing the pain,
And creating freedom in my brain.

Smell

Why do you give me such a hassle?
Every time we have a battle.
All I wish for is a fresh breeze,
Pink petals and friendly honeybees.

When you appear in my life,
I feel that in my heart is a sharp knife.
Pain and anger are taking over,
I wish I had a magic clover.

I am sorry for the rejection,
I am pleading for correction.
Please forgive and set me free,
I am sorry for the 'dead sea'.

I am standing here and facing you,
I hope my love will come through.
I don't understand this confusion,
'Dear child' allow me the solution.

It is Divinity, in whom I believe,
And I will love you until you leave.
Please forgive me for holding on,
Please forgive me for the black dawn.

It feels like a huge tornado,
It is stirring up trouble and woe.
I am sorry, please let go,
Thank you for this chance to grow.

What is going on inside
Why am I pushing me aside?
Why do I fear to love 'I'?
Why is it so hard to apply?

Last night I looked into your eyes,
And I felt love instead of lies.
Transmutation from anger to light,
For this moment there is no fight.

As I am gently rocking in this glory
I am just am, and there is no story.
I breathe in the aromas of the roses,
'The golden key' comes and proposes.

This doesn't mean that I know,
I have no idea of the woe,
I keep cleaning when doubts appear,
Thank you for loving me my dear.

Burden

I am tired of carrying this load,
How can I crack this code?
The roots are heavy and deep,
And the stairs are very steep.

I feel the origins can be undone,
And there is no need to run.
As I stare into the radiant sunset,
I ask my child to help me to reset.

My mind is contaminated
With the rubbish I accumulated.
It is a conflict within my soul,
And what I see is a bag of coal.

I am sorry, please forgive me,
It is time to let go, don't you see?
Erase the whole 'burden show'
And my breathing will flow and grow.

Suddenly I feel a fresh boost,
Something inside of me reduced.
I now see flowers blooming within,
Inner peace is here to stay and win.

I am grateful for this awakening sight,
And loosening up what was tight.
Thank you for erasing this illusion,
I can enjoy my present without confusion.

War

When I panic and am in pain
It takes over my soul and vein.
I am tired, oh such a waste
Of suffering in this stuck space.

It is like burning alive
And there is no chance to survive.
I feel weak in my mind,
Please don't leave me behind.

Clean and clean are the aims
To put out the damaging flames,
My poor soul is in despair
And I can't handle this 'raging flare'.

Please dear 'child' let it go,
I am sorry that I built this woe
Between my mind, body and soul,
That took over 'I', the purest creation of all.

I love you so much, dear thought.
Please let go of this tight knot.
I am sorry I kept you inside,
Thank you for being my guide.

It is a war I want to win,
And put the battleship in the bin.
Nobody else will do it for me,
I am alone in this journey.

I now see this battle will be fair,
I need to step up and be here.
Protect my mind, body and heart,
With peace and love; the war will depart.

I will love this war to death
And I am ready to take the first step.
Cherishing the indigo blue glove,
It is 100% responsibility in love.

Rage

Now you are here at present,
I want to get rid of your scent.
I cannot handle you; it's taking its toll,
It is getting out of control.

I am cleaning with continuation
Without fear or expectation,
How can I melt away the toxic thoughts?
Right now, rage is calling the shots.

Horrible feelings going on inside,
And I clean until the sun leaves the sky.
Then more cleaning through the night
And it continues when the sunrays light.

You are still here and torturing
My mind, my body and my being,
I am stuck in this disgusting dirt,
The raging handcuffs really hurt.

I am sorry for this pain and rigidity,
Please forgive me Divinity.
I love you forever and ever more,
Thank you for letting go of this war.

I choose to be light and pure,
Please help me to find the cure.
Please forgive me, I love you,
Thank you for the breakthrough.

Now my life is such a delight,
I am grateful that I survived the fight.
Past memories are sliding with ease,
I switch on the light and hug the trees.

Money

Is it dirty or is it clean?
Is it pink or is it green?
Is it white or is it blue?
Is it loose or is it glue?

Is it love or is it pain?
Is it loss or is it gain?
Is it weak or is it strong?
Is it right or is it wrong?

Is it love or is it hate?
Is it small or is it great?
Is it something you really crave?
Does it make you scared or brave?

Is it easy or is it hard?
What is the belief that you regard?
Is it here or kept at bay?
Do you save or blow it away?

Is it stuck or is it flow?
Is it nothing or is it a woe?
Is it you or is it other?
Is it that you never bother?

Is it often or rarely peaks?
Is it that it never seeks?
Is it attending or embark?
Is it fades away in the dark?

Free your mind and money will flow
In abundance and shining glow,
The door will open with a blue sky
As you bid expectations a goodbye.

Now it is your turn to choose,
What money really means for you?
Where is it that you want to be?
Your mind is the one which holds the key.

Business

Are you big or are you small?
Are you happy or do you fall?
Are you blocked or do you flow?
What is it that you stand for?

Are you alone or with friends?
Are you old or up with trends?
Are you loving or being grumpy?
Is your path smooth or bumpy?

Do you flourish like a flower?
Are you sweet or are you sour?
Are you above or below?
Are you fast or walking slow?

Are you proud or are you shy?
Are you shut or do you fly?
Are you complete or are you empty?
Are you kind or peak green with envy?

What is it you are fighting for?
Do you lose or do you score?
Do you know your aim and vision?
Or do you live in a dark prison?

What is it you choose to see?
Are you here or will you flee?
Do you see yourself in the stars?
Or are you holding up any bars?

Your thoughts are always inside,
They will show up and never hide.
You can ignore them; it's your fate,
You can be stuck or in a clear state.

Unclear goal and empty desire,
It is a problem set on fire.
Cement your core and your soul,
Let the Love in you take control.

Stubbornness

Sometimes when two hearts
Don't know where love starts,
All they can do is let go,
This will put an end to their woe.

How come we are too proud?
Why do we fear love and feel doubt?
How come that we want to love
And the door to our hearts is shut?

Let in love and feel the breeze,
Feel the movement and the ease.
Feel your soul and purity,
Please forgive me Divinity.

I am sorry for being stubborn,
I am sorry for creating this wall of prison.
I am sorry for being stuck inside,
I am sorry for the pain I supplied.

Please help me to let go,
Release, clean and heal my soul.
I now understand and can see
How I open my love to thee.

I closed myself inside for years.
Now it is time to release the fears.
I welcome all the joys instead,
And let inspirations be spread.

I will nurture the light in my space,
So everyone will be in a right place.
The Cosmos gets whatever it needs,
Peace, love and golden beads.

Reaction

It is grey and gloomy inside,
Anger, pain, panic and divide.
Every experience is an illusion,
It stirs up trouble and confusion.

This reaction shook my world,
My body, mind and soul whirled.
'I' didn't realise it back then,
It was a chance to create Zen.

Today as 'I' was helping a friend,
Who is grieving and at a dead end.
The memory of the shock came back,
It was time to release the toxic plaque.

'I' was preparing the red rose,
'I' realised it was time to close.
Wasn't sure what to think or say,
It was a grey and gloomy day.

'I' asked for forgiveness and peace,
So the blame and anger can cease.
'I' asked for love and healing light,
And put an end to the heavy fright.

My body and mind were apart,
My heart was struck with a dart.
My happiness faded and I cried,
I felt my soul left me and died.

This reaction is making me see,
Now I can be happy and be me.
I switch on my light and shine,
My life became a goldmine.

The golden key of knowledge,
No uncertainty and blockage.
Reacting from love and clarity,
It is the route to prosperity.

Expectations

I don't expect the sun to rise,
It will be light when I open my eyes.
I don't expect the stars to shine,
It is their job at night to align.

I don't expect the air to escape,
It comes to me in every shape.
I don't expect time to flee,
It passes by without a plea.

I don't expect the cows to speak,
I don't expect the flowers to bleed.
I don't expect a sudden rain,
I don't expect to be in pain.

Do I expect money or results?
Do I expect rights or faults?
Do I expect to fall or rise?
Do I expect smiles or cries?

Do I expect to hide or be?
Do I expect to be blind or see?
Do I expect the lack or have?
Do I expect to understand my 'crap'?

Do I expect a good report?
Do I expect a ball in my court?
Do I expect to be in the flow?
Do I expect a heavy blow?

Do I expect my soul to heal,
Without cleaning it for real?
Do I expect to have clarity
Without taking responsibility?

Being responsible is the key,
We can be stuck or free.
All is alive and it is within,
My job is to get out of the spin.

Let go of the toxic thoughts,
Transform all the heavy knots.
Inspirations is what follows,
I set myself free from my sorrows.

There will be an empty space,
It will be no data or fast race.
Remember the purpose of 'I',
It is freedom and I light up the sky.

Chapter Two: The Link to the Source

When I was younger, experiencing and living in a not so stable environment, I always looked outside of myself. I understood the drama, trauma, abuse and violence that were taking place, but I felt it was outside of me. In fact what I could see physically was outside of myself, but my emotions and thoughts were not. These were hiding within me and I locked them away for many, many years in my subconscious mind. Some might call it non-conscious mind, others call it their inner child and some call it the Holy Spirit. As I was holding or storing these emotions they just kept accumulating year after year, until one day I received a phone call that destroyed my life. My inner child's hard drive overloaded and I had to make a decision to reset my life.

I learnt to love my inner child, care for and nurture its beauty and ask it for help when I needed it. It is my best business partner who helps me to create freedom. I also noticed that my physical wellbeing changed as my mind transformed.

When we carry something mentally that exceeds what we are capable of we can overexert ourselves and we will be unable to function mentally, which subsequently will affect our physical and material life.

Close your eyes and gently discover that you have someone within who needs your love and loves you more than you can imagine.

Don't search for me, I am here; I was always here waiting for you to love me. 'I' love you.

Subconscious Mind

What are you, you poor soul?
Are you separate or are you whole?
I have been far away from you,
But I can see now what is true.

Rage, anger, annoyance and murder,
Sadness, grief, death and torture,
Backstabbing, abuse and fears,
I love you until the light appears.

The blurry screen that you show,
Frustrations inside that can blow,
Jealousy, greed and business woes,
Questions that made you froze.

The problem is always within,
Not outside and not in the bin.
We decide if we want to hold on,
Or let the memories be gone.

I love you with all my heart,
Forgive me for the bad start.
Gently release the fear and hurt,
Let go of the frustration and dirt.

These illusions in front of my eyes,
Are the acceptance of control and cries.
It is the database I filled up and built,
I am the one who nurtured my guilt.

Please forgive me for the stress,
I am responsible for the mess.
I will care for you forever more,
You are my true love whom I adore.

Chapter Three: Freedom

During my healing process I learnt that the sole purpose of letting go of these thoughts and emotions was that I was going to be FREE of them and not for the purpose of expectations. Many people make the mistake when erasing their emotions that they think that they will receive something huge or win the lottery. They are focusing on expectations, which can be like an 'iron grip' that holds us prisoners, rather than simply loving what is. There are three reasons I love this problem solving technique so much and they are:

1) **My unwanted thought/ emotion is only an illusion.**

2) **I don't even have to go into the problem to solve it.**

3) **It instantly creates freedom.**

As I was letting go of various emotions and past memories I started to feel lighter, my vision was clearer and I started to regain clarity and awareness of my being. As a consequence I created and manifested my goals, dreams and desires. I attracted people, who are now my dear friends, into my life, who helped and guided me along this difficult path. The transformation in me was/is continuous up until today and I keep learning about myself at every moment. I am grateful for each experience and opportunity to create freedom within.

Whilst you are reflecting on these poems you might notice yourself opening up like a flower, that is waking up at dawn and the crystal clear dewdrops are running through its blossoms. Remember harmony, freedom and happiness is within you and you are able to reach inside and create it at your wish. I would like to finish off with a quote, which means when we are committed to take 100% responsibility for what is going on in our life, when we accept the love within, we will create inspirations and freedom.

"Take my hand and love

'I' show you enlightenment

Freedom will appear."

Love

What are you little spark?
Are you green, white or dark?
Is it something you lacked in the past,
Is it that you were never asked?

I give you my love dear 'child',
Loving you is gentle and mild.
Soft love and gentle cuddles,
It will clear the muddy puddles.

Allowing my love to come to you,
It means that nothing is a taboo.
I collected the problems within,
With love transformations will begin.

I look at you and open my heart.
You are the best buddy at the start.
I am grateful that you never cease,
And guide me to be in peace.

This love is pure and simple,
You are my heart's temple.
Wealth, health, joy and freedom,
You connect to that kingdom.

Changes

Hello, I am here in this mess again,
Who will help me to unplug the drain?
Not sure what to do or how to start.
Another 'mortgage' comes into the cart.

Let me win you over,
So you can be my lover.
This chaos within,
Is like a slow killing.

It is full and stuffy,
I want a chance to feel fluffy.
Be gentle and care for me,
Release all my negativity.

Suddenly something starts to spark,
My pain eases and I ask:
"What was I holding inside?"
Was it black or blue? I can't decide.

I stroke you with my tender arm,
Let go of the heaviness; be calm
And what was hard, it becomes light.
I am so grateful, my miraculous delight.

Letting Go

I have been harbouring my woes inside,
Heartbreak, pain, suffering and cries.
And whatever was going on in the past;
Confusion, unloving, hates and lies.

Back then, I didn't know that I can let go,
The traffic lights were red and slow.
I was not allowed to show what I feel,
And I never believed it was real.

I dreamt of a future with love that lasts,
What is a life with violent blasts?
I kept my grief and tears inside,
I just wanted to escape and hide.

And one day my mind had the insight,
"I've had enough of the abuse and fight!"
I made a decision and got my bag,
Left the only world I thought I had.

When it was time, I had to part,
And it really broke my heart.
I didn't look back to the dark past,
I was moving forward very fast.

I discovered a whole new world,
Met new people and their twirl,
Although the most important of all,
Was 'I', my one and only soul.

While I was getting to know 'I',
I learnt that it's ok to let go and smile.
It is ok to be sad sometimes,
We learn from it, and put it behind.

As long as I let go and move on,
My life transforms into freedom.
I love being in the flow,
No attachments and no woe.

I am now cleaning to be free
Without expectations and any 'fee'.
This burden has now been lifted
And my life is wonderfully gifted.

My dreams of a happy life,
It is brimming with love and not strife.
That little girl who lived in fear
Now let go, still believes and sees clear!

Chapter Four: Inspirations

Like I mentioned in the previous chapter I learnt some tools that I was able to use to heal myself. Some of them are Reiki, Law of Attraction, Tapas Acupressure Technique (TAT), Emotional Freedom Technique and Ho'oponopono, which means to correct an error, which is what inspired this poem book.

The most important message was for me to eliminate expectations and allow my goals, dreams and desires to enter my life naturally. What it means is being in the flow, and without any force or pressure inspirations started to appear in my life. Inspirations can appear in the form of an idea, answer, vision or anything really. We may expect our desire to appear from a certain direction and as a consequence we can shut down other avenues.

Because inspired results always appeared from the least expected places I learnt to just embrace them and be grateful for every delight in my life. I actually use an exercise I call the 'power of gratitude', which you might have heard of. Each day I spend my time being grateful for what I already have, for example: that I am living, that I can see, walk and hear. That I can breathe fresh air and have a home, a bed to sleep in and drink clean water. Just by doing this exercise I start my day appreciating and loving who I already am. In this chapter you will be able to discover the trust and faith in yourself.

Your inner power and resilience that made you into this incredible warrior that you are.

> *"Because you have seen Me, you have believed, blessed are those who have not seen, and yet believed."*

(John 20:29)

Divinity

The most wonderful feeling of all,
It is when divinity appears at my call.
There is absolutely 'nothing',
My soul is in peace and loving.

I am in a hub of joy and sparks,
The Cosmos is making its marks.
I am on the top of the mountain,
The water is pure in God's fountain.

I am so grateful to be free,
I cherish the 'inspiration tree'.
Pure light is filled in my heart,
And I know this is only a start.

My soul is filled with gratitude,
I love my zero 'attitude'.
My Universe is buzzing,
Life is good in nothing.

Inspirations

Can be there and can be here,
Can be out and can be near.
Can be green or can be yellow,
Can be sweet or can be mellow.

Can be love and can be happy,
Can be miracle and can be beauty.
Can be new or can be old,
Can be what you've never been told.

Can be deep or can be shallow,
It can be something that you swallow.
Can be heavy or can be light,
Can be what you feel is right.

Can be up or can be down,
Can be anywhere in town.
Can be usual or can be rare,
It can be something that you wear.

Inspirations are shining gold,
So act on what will unfold.
Within the mind, body and soul,
That is when 'I' will be a whole.

Sometimes it is a hard defence,
And not everything makes sense.
The only purpose of existence
Is to be responsible with consistence.

That is when inspirations flow,
From nothing there will be a glow.
Continue the cleaning and be free,
Live life from inspirations and just be.

Just for Today

Just for today let it be peace,
Just for today let the war cease.
Just for today I will be me,
Just for today I will love thee.

Just for today I choose to let go,
Just for today my heart will glow.
Just for today let it be serenity,
Just for today I love my identity.

Just for today I cherish my soul,
Just for today I rock and roll.
Just for today I clean my errors,
Just for today I stop my terrors.

Just for today I promise you this,
I will clean and then find the bliss.
Just for today I embrace 'I',
Just for today I love the blue sky.

Faith

When the tide is really high
And you can't see the blue sky.
What will keep you alive?
Who will help you to survive?

One word showed me the light,
It was faith, which kept me bright.
I almost forgot, and was blind,
That it was already in my mind.

Thank you for this magical word,
Even though my thoughts were stirred,
Patted me on the back and said:
"Love and you will be ahead."

There I was with my head bowed,
A miracle appeared behind the cloud.
The answer was right there,
I was grateful for this magical air.

Sometimes when I get hurt,
I let inside the chaotic dirt.
I am grateful to be light and clean,
I wiped everything off the screen.

Father, mother, child as one,
Unite together in the bright sun.
Working in the flow within,
And keep emptying the bin.

The power inside 'I' is my aid,
What I learnt will never fade.
Love 'I' – that is the mission,
Forgive and let go all suspicion.

Seeing with the Eyes of God

As I was cleaning on memory lane
And was emptying my drain
My eyes glanced at 'My Wild Irish Rose'
And I instantly knew what 'I' disclose.

See people with 'Divine Love',
Take off the judgmental glove.
All our problems are within,
Forgive and get out of this spin.

I kept on cleaning and seeing people,
Then I stepped into your steeple.
I saw the whole Universe in front of me
And I whispered: "Let Divinity's Love Be."

I saw a huge crane appearing
And 'my child' was cheering.
I felt my eyes were tearing
And the memories were cleaning.

Then I saw him, who 'stole her soul',
Who 'destroyed her and left a deep hole'.
I asked: "How can I see the God in him?"
Then I saw the volcano dim.

And it was calm and love so pure,
Everything was clear, and I knew the cure.
The whole cosmos is a 'Perfect Place',
The mountain to be on is Divinity's base.

Seeing others with the eyes of God,
The silence was present and I awed.
The world became peaceful and perfect,
I understood the power of respect.

Closing Cycle

Another cycle of my life is over
I won't hide under grass or clover,
Those days are detached and gone,
And I wake up to a new dawn.

It feels free, fresh and peaceful,
The Universe is looking graceful.
My mind is light and in a void,
All the memories are destroyed.

Pleasant breeze and the sun is warm,
I love to stand on this platform.
I open myself to the Universal light,
I wrap myself in blue, green and white.

My path is the same, only a new era,
I am happy to be on this Riviera.
I bathe in the sound of the sea.
My love within will set me free.

Chapter Five: Law of Attraction, Words & Vibes

Another powerful tool I've learnt whilst resetting my life was the Law of Attraction. As I was completing my Life Coaching Diploma I came across this topic. I saw the movie that was created about this subject and I started to research trainers and teachers. I guess by the powers of Law of Attraction I met Michael Losier, who wrote the book: Law of Attraction, The Science of Attracting More of What You Want and Less of What You Don't, who appeared on Oprah's radio show and is still training and facilitating seminars across the world; he trained me to become a Certified Law of Attraction Facilitator.

When I first read his book I instantly started to use the tools and techniques and I must say it worked in every area of my life. I travelled to Phoenix in 2009 to take the course and have been training people ever since. In the following chapters I will be writing about what the Law of Attraction is, our words, thoughts, vibrations and values. I will be writing about relationships, forgiveness and compassion. Then I will move onto our goals, dreams and desires including the source of abundance. As it benefited my clients I will share my own Law of Attraction techniques that I hope you will find useful.

When we use our words it is always good to be precise and be aware of what are we saying. What we talk about we bring about; in other words we create our existence with our words, thoughts and feelings. We might not think we are using 'The Laws of Attraction' or we might have never heard of it, although it is working in our life right now.

Law of Attraction is in us and we are in control whether we are aware, believe it or not. What I love about it is that some of my clients took a more scientific approach, some a spiritual route and some adjusted the tools and techniques the way it worked for them the best. That is the beauty in the tools: that you use the one that works for you in line with your own beliefs.

Since I was very young I have loved writing poems and after a recent spring clean in my mind, home and in my digital world I found some poems that reflected sadness, suffering and pain. I looked at those poems with love, because they taught me gratitude, inner peace, kindness, abundance and happiness. I was delighted that those feelings were completely detached from my existence and now I understand that they were only illusions that I chose to write about and that attracted more of the same.

How can we transform unwanted thoughts to our natural state of mind and most importantly to the results we want? First of all let me tell you that thoughts have no power unless we give life to them. When we wish to erase a thought that somehow we became attached to the first thing is to ask ourselves: **"So what do I want?"**

I remember someone told me at a seminar that she wants to be rich so I asked her how many times in the day is she sending out the vibration of abundance; she said zero, instead she was pondering and worrying about her financial situation. She realised that what she did and thought of was not what she wanted and kept attracting quite the opposite. Slowly she started to focus on a thought of abundance and sent out the vibrations of what abundance meant to her, and then she was able to transform her results into a positive one. This is how simple it is to erase and create more of what we want. Really she just wanted to be happy!

What happens is that subconsciously we create a story that we don't want. We make the mistake of becoming involved with our unwanted words, thoughts and feelings and therefore we create a whirlpool of problems that keeps bubbling away until it eventually explodes and can affect our physical, mental, material, business and spiritual life.

In order to attract something that we want, we have to release what we are already holding on to. Then naturally our feelings and results will change.

You are the remote control of your desires!

What is Law of Attraction?

Whether you believe it or not,
Whether you think little or a lot.
Whether you smile or cry,
Whether you're down or up in the sky.

Whether you give attention to love,
Whether you want to be above.
Whether you focus on your foe,
Whether you want to scream or blow.

Whether your mind is in peace,
Whether you want war to cease.
Whether you are in a good mood,
Whether you are happy or rude.

You can only attract what is in you,
And your feelings are the clue.
We have feelings at every second,
Listen, feel and see your heaven.

What is Law of Attraction's Job?

Everyone enjoys the air,
When they feel like a funfair!
Bright, colourful and happy,
Get what they want and feel ready.

Wherever they go they lift up the air,
Whether it is grey, dark or not fair.
So my friend I am asking you too,
Be the same and uplift your mood.

When you understand your positive vibe,
You can inspire men, women and child.
If you give your attention to negative,
That is what you will receive.

I know a wise man once he told me
Always be careful of your energy!
Nurture yourself and take care,
Then you will achieve whatever you dare.

If you attract a negative vibe,
Be responsible – don't judge or hide.
That is there because of you,
So understand what you need to do.

It can be there, it can be here,
Be vigilant of what you will hear.
It will unfold and orchestrate
And match your Universal state.

Words, Thoughts and Results

When I have something to describe
I am always sending out a vibe.
I craft my words and create my thoughts,
I gather the letters and cross the dots.

I open my heart to let in the good,
I let go of would, should and could.
I embrace my results that I receive,
I adore the moment of sparkling eve.

My feelings are getting into the groove,
And my results can only improve.
I vibrate my dreams and let them shine,
They are nobody else's, but mine.

I am responsible for my thinking,
I love it when my goals are linking.
Letting go of all questions and grind,
I will manifest clarity in my mind.

Love, peace, happiness and health,
Joy, harmony, balance and wealth,
Confidence, success and laughter,
These words are sought after.

As I am standing on the top of a hill,
I feel one with nature and my will.
There is a magic vibe in the breeze
Re-creating will come with ease.

If I think that something is wrong,
And negative thoughts come along,
I hit the reset button within me,
And let my vibrations just be free.

Don't, Not and No

When I think of my dreams
I set up some sturdy beams.
When I speak of my desire,
I dress it in clean attire.

It is easy to be stuck in a rut,
But there are words I can cut.
What words can stop the flow?
They are don't, not and no.

When I feel that I want to cry
I smile and dry up my eye.
When I want to give up and go,
I reframe the word so I can flow.

When I am fed up and don't want to wait.
I use a different word to change my state.
When I see that my purse is empty,
I use proof that there is plenty.

When I am angry and I can't see
I open my eye and I find a key.
When I say that I don't want to trust,
I create faith and shake off my dust.

When I say I don't want fight,
I create words that show me the light.
When I think that I have no land,
I reach out with a positive hand.

When I hear my thoughts slam,
It makes me realise who I really am.
When I say that I don't like changes
I know positive comes in many ranges.

The question that is in a bold font:
"So what is it that I really want?"
I don't say that I can't glow
I attract my journey and dare to grow.

Chapter Six: Relationships

When I was growing up I experienced many different types of relationships and at times I was heartbroken. As I child I was not aware what the real meaning of forgiveness and compassion was. I felt let down by many people including my nearest and dearest. I now see it in a different light and have compassion towards those people who caused me the most traumatic experiences.

What made me change my mind? How did I become who I am from the victim to the survivor, a warrior and a fighter? In certain traumatic situations I was unable to protect myself as a child so letting go of the pain was difficult for me. As I grew stronger and started to heal I was able to teach or train people how to treat me. I simply detached from those who weren't in vibrational harmony with me as it was causing me stress and unhappiness. When we hold onto someone that is contaminating our overall vibration we will attract more of the same.

The anger, pain and sadness were within me and as I was holding onto them I kept attracting more of the same negative relationships that reflected my past. In the end I just wanted to be happy! I learnt to create my happy relationships – starting with myself.

It is easy to blame others for our stress or anger and when we feel guilty about someone we can carry that burden for years just because of our thoughts which are only illusions that we created. Either way the only person who is suffering is us.

Forgiveness comes from within and it means that we change the way we see something and what we are looking at will change, but in reality what changed? Just you!

Have you heard of your vibrational meter reader? If you haven't I can tell you that you have one within you and that is your feelings. When you meet someone for the first time you can feel a bit of resistance or get on with them like you've known each other for many years. I met this lovely lady in my local Sainsbury's and we connected instantly. She is always cheerful and happy, and cares about her job and customers. I sent a letter to the CEO of Sainsbury's to let him know how wonderful his worker is. He sent me a lovely reply and the next time I saw Claire I told her it was me that sent the email. She said she was short of money that week and received a £30 voucher from her employer; I think she said they call it a 'love card' and she was able to buy what she wanted. When she told me the story it filled me with happiness. We were/are in the same vibrational harmony and both attracted more abundance into our life.

Naturally we are not always in harmony with our partner, neighbours, clients, friends, family members or even with ourselves. Our vibrational meter reader is telling us that the other person might be less positive and therefore we are not on the same dial or frequency with them. However hard we try we just can't get along with them and the relationship breaks down. Of course this doesn't necessarily mean they are bad people.

We can ask them to talk about what they actually want, which will create a more positive atmosphere and at the same time increase their vibrational dial. Therefore both parties will be talking about what they want and sending the vibrations the way they want them to be.

People react from the thoughts that they believe are true in their mind and our reactions to that determine our vibrational frequency. The idea is to mind/nurture our own vibration and detach from their unwanted thoughts and stories. It is good to stay in our own business and in that way we won't get tangled or attached to anyone else's.

I also believe that with compassion and forgiveness we will notice how our vibration will stay positive and we will attract the happy relationships we want more of.

Flourish from within and let love
come to you at every moment.

Relationships

It can be tricky and it can be long,
It can be weak or it can be strong.
It can be true and it can be fake,
It can be healthy or it can ache.

It can be sadness and it can be joy,
It can be happy and it can annoy.
It can be anger and it can be hate,
It can be love and it can be fate.

What is the best way to decide
How to keep on the right side?
What can I do to attract the one?
Who will match my vibrational fun?

How to find my ideal clients,
Where are those wonderful giants?
How can I create balance with friends?
What if there can't be amends?

What do I do with spoilt relations?
How can I stop my frustrations?
How do I teach my brother to love?
Will he eliminate his boxing glove?

How do I teach my husband to see?
Will he ever understand my plea?
What can I do to make him hear?
Shall I scream the answer to his ear?

In the process of an ideal attraction,
Good to find a matching vibration.
And if it is not and I feel low,
I am giving my dial a blow.

I allow how others will treat me,
I can choose to be happy or flee.
I let go of expectations and smile,
I mind my energy in style.

When people know what they desire,
It creates harmony and reaches higher.
The communication will become easy,
It will be blossoming, light and breezy.

I release all my expectations
And set up secure foundations.
I nurture the love and light in me,
I accept, tolerate and I am free to be.

Clients

They know that you are there,
Their minds hide and stare,
Some live in silence, some with scare,
Making the first step – would they dare?

Some want change, some want nothing,
Some reject and some accepting,
Some anxious and some depressing,
Some stressed and some believing.

What is the reason for fading away?
Why are you keeping change at bay?
What stops you from being 'You'?
What is the reason? Don't have a clue?

What is your aim, what is your trouble?
Are you in crisis or ignoring your muddle?
What is the reason you are not facing?
What is the reason you are resisting?

Are you afraid of opening 'You'?
Are you afraid of facing the truth?
Are you scared of letting go?
Are you scared of going with the flow?

What makes you run away?
What makes you stop each day?
What makes you shiver and in shock?
What is giving you that block?

Facing challenges along the road
Is what makes you strong and bold.
If you want to create your being inside,
You must take responsibility and not hide.

Clear and let go with no defence.
Love and forgiveness will commence.
Your being will transform into pure light
And you will discover the 'miracle' of life.

Conversation within

Leave me alone, I am fed up
With all the rubbish that comes up.
I want you to love me gently,
Hug me; please don't hurt me.

Just hush up and listen to thee,
Stop creating anymore 'mind spree'.
Love me with your tender heart,
And don't rip me apart.

I am happy that you are ready to start.
Your warmth and love reaches my heart,
Release the hurt with a big smile
Thank you for the reconcile.

This will be a great friendship,
Let's stick together on our future trip.
The best business partner I can wish for,
My dear soul, I love you ever more.

Chapter Seven: Dreams, Goals & Desires

As we journey through our life we make some plans and would like to achieve and create more of the results we want. Be it our ideal money, health, weight, clients, love, inner peace, car, house, job or any other desires.

Remember what I said about thoughts becoming problems; they only become problems if we give life to them. In order to create clarity you will have to identify what it is that you really want. Even if you are not sure what you want you can easily create clarity just by flipping it on its head by asking yourself: if I don't want that what do I want instead? Therefore by observing contrast briefly you are giving birth to clarity. How do we know what briefly is? Briefly means it is up to you how long you will tolerate something that doesn't make you feel good. Some people can hold onto confusion for years, because they feel comfortable in that state of mind.

Are you uncomfortable enough to create clarity and transform your goals into results? Remember if your current situation doesn't make you feel good you are sending out negative vibrations and 'Law of Attraction' is giving you more of the same. The source of abundance starts and is in you. How many times in the day are you including abundance in your words and thoughts? What is it that you are affirming about your dreams, goals and desires to yourself? I would like to quote my teacher and mentor Michael Losier:

> *"Abundance is a feeling. Be more deliberate to include the feeling of abundance in your current vibration – your Vibrational Bubble."*

There is a saying that we can't see the wood for the trees. We are trying to figure out the outcome. We lose sight of what is important and can get side-tracked with unimportant details. Therefore we might feel stressed, pressured or even angry. With a clear mind we will be able to follow and create more of our dreams, goals and desires that will make us happy!

> *Staying in the present will help you to create a happy and abundant life.*

Identifying Desires

When I want to identify my desire,
I observe contrast that sets me on fire.
Although it is for a short while
It gives me clarity and makes me smile.

Contrast doesn't makes me feel good,
It can be anger, hate or a bad mood.
The trick is to observe it fast
So it can give our mind a blast.

What is it that I really want?
Is it blue, pink or to flaunt?
Clarification, it's an ideal tool,
I stand strong on my stool.

When I create my mind's clear space,
My soul will be in a better place.
Understanding the goals of my heart
It offers me an uplifting start.

I write my list and I feel my goals,
I eliminate all the bad holes.
I feel the peace where I belong,
I love my life and I stay strong.

Vibrational Bubble

What can I include in my bubble?
Will it be easy or will I have trouble?
Will I achieve my desires in an instant?
Will it be near or will it be distant?

My dreams and goals are still outside,
Because my vibration is not applied.
In order to include them in my bubble,
I have to send my vibes in double.

Daydreaming or complaining is the same,
It gets included in the bubble's game.
Send the vibrations the way I want it to be,
I create my vision of a beautiful sea.

I hear the sound of my new car,
I jump for joy when I see a star.
I create my vision board of beauty,
I am grateful that my life is fruity.

I see myself joyful and in peace,
I leave the anger and fear to cease.
I fill my bubble with pure love,
My vibrations will rise above.

Affirmations

It can be healthy or slim,
It can be bright or dim.
It can be clever or dark,
It can be peaceful or a bark.

I can be happy or sad,
I can be good or bad.
I can be pretty or ugly
I can be flat or bubbly.

I can be sour or sweet,
I can be cold or a treat.
It can be rich or humble,
It can be a torte or a crumble.

It can be weak or broken,
It can be out or unspoken.
It can be silent or loud,
It can be holy or proud.

Existing in the process
Gives me a good progress
I am attracting my bond
And the Universe will respond.

Chapter Eight: Allowing – 'Be the Source You Want to See'

Allowing is the absence of doubt and doubt is a negative vibration, therefore we have to allow more and doubt less. That is all there is to it; there are no secrets or other tricky routes to allowing.

We are the creators of our life and we can choose whatever it is that we wish to be, to see or to hear. We might want to allow love, peace, abundance, happiness, health, wealth, ideal clients, increased profits, holidays, a beautiful car, a new home, children or success or I could go on.

We already have anything that we desire within. All we have to do is to be open to allow and receive it. Often people tell me that they are not sure what their life's purpose is or how can they find/allow it. I tell them that determining our purpose in life depends on how willing we are to take 100% responsibility for what is going on within. I will give you an example. I met someone for a coffee and as we were talking, she revealed the trauma she had been through in the past month. She was unable to allow her desires, because she was not willing to take responsibility for what was going on in her life. She told me: "Andrea 'I' just want to be happy!" I asked her what she thought was stopping her from being that and she said it was her own thoughts and doubts. She felt confused, fed up and had had enough of her current situation. I met her a few months after that and she told me that she had let go of her burden and her life was much happier now.

When we understand who we are within and are willing to let go of our doubts we will create freedom and results or inspirations.

Also, it is good to understand and be clear what freedom and results mean for us. For example, for me freedom means that 'I' am just am. I am in my natural state of mind.

Results or we can call them inspirations – for me it means that 'I' am in the flow – I am responsible for what is going on within and allowing what is already mine to appear in my life.

When we experience the beauty of freedom we won't even have to think about results; they will express themselves in ways that we won't even realise and as I mentioned before they come from the least expected source.

By being responsible and nurturing our foundation we are nurturing a treasure chest of our desires that we are holding the golden key to and it is waiting for us to love, discover and reach for it. Go on, grab your key to allowing and just be happy!

Spread your wings and learn to fly; open your mind and be one with who you are.

Allowing

Allowing is the absence of doubt,
I let the questions fade right out.
I embrace the gifts I receive,
And celebrate what I achieve.

I allow time for proof to appear
And cherish it with a big cheer.
I celebrate my attractions and vibes,
And I refuse the ego's bribes.

And when expectations are arising,
The problems are not surprising.
I can't figure out the how and when
I let the Universe bring me a Zen.

I allow the abundance to come to me,
I love the eagles and the blue sea.
I have what I want, it is within,
And my doubts can go to the bin.

When I felt the beauty in the stars,
My poem was sent up to Mars.
When my ideal home was written down,
I moved into my perfect town.

I allow the love to enter,
I place my light in the centre.
I forgive and let go my woe,
I am open to where I will go.

A lot can happen at any time,
It can be peace or just a dime.
I trust the attraction in my heart,
I let the Universe create my art.

Be the Source You Want to See

I love when I can open my mind,
I see the world as being kind.
Sunshine and nature together,
I am enjoying this beautiful weather.

I see the world in so many ways,
Feel the vibrations and the rays.
Hear the music of my heart,
My wishes can easily start.

Teach my wisdom across the earth,
People will listen and see their worth.
Create positive words and thoughts,
Reset my love and ease my knots.

Whether it is raining or lightning,
Or if I think something is frightening.
When I change my mind inside,
I will be doubtless and glide.

I live my life the way I want it to be,
I give a chance to wind, fire, earth and sea.
When my life took a wonderful turn,
I was given a second chance to return.

When I think something is not right,
I let go and embrace the light.
Rainbows will appear in the sky
And I will be ready to let go and fly.

Chapter Nine: Tips & Techniques

I would like to share with you some techniques that I have found useful to let go of my emotions, doubts and worries. Some might match your communication style better than others and you might share with someone who will benefit from them. Feel free to apply these as you wish; you can add or take away from them. The idea is to make it work for you.

Step Aside – When we are not in balance the smallest of issues will feel like huge problems and it can contaminate our wellbeing. You can do this exercise standing up and also in your mind. I personally prefer to do it standing up, but it depends what works for you.

Close your eyes and think of the problem you want to solve. Then say it in your mind or out loud: I now heal this thought, the story that I created and the emotions I am experiencing. I release and heal everything in my mind, body, soul, vibration and my Universe that is connected to this. I send love and peace to myself and to anyone who participated in this thought. Dear thought, I am grateful that you appeared in my life, I understand that you are only here for me to learn and move forward in the now.

When you think it is right for you, simply 'Step Aside' from the position you were standing in. Shake and detach yourself from the problem physically. Embrace what you want instead of what you just waved goodbye to. Feel, hear and see it within – you already have it.

Motivation Mountain – I love this technique, because we are not only erasing the problem, but we also create something positive. Whatever negative feeling, thought, emotion, words or images appear in front of you, simply push them off a cliff. See, feel or hear that the problem explodes, breaks into pieces or simply disappears into thin air. After that you can choose to think of what you want instead. After practising this exercise my clients told me that they felt they had this incredible power that emerged from inside and after destroying their thoughts they saw positive images such as a rainbow, sunshine or sailing boats carrying away the burdens. It is up to the individual's mind.

Shredder – The good old shredder technique comes in handy; especially if you do a lot of shredding then it will be a walk in the park for you. Simply put your thought that causes you discomfort through a shredder mentally or physically. Tailor it the way you wish.

Magnet of Love – Imagine that you have a magnet in front of you, behind you, next to you on both sides, below your feet and above your head, so you are in the middle of these huge magnets. Then imagine, feel or hear that these magnets are pulling out all your negative thoughts, feelings, and negative people around you, toxins and everything in connection to what you are experiencing. Softly let everything go with love and gratitude; it was there for you to learn and grow, but this will help you to create space for new attractions and allow your desires.

Vibrational Bubble Shelves – For this exercise's sake let's say that there is this bubble around you and you are in the middle. The vibrations/feelings that you are experiencing (good or bad) are accumulating on your shelves in your vibrational bubble. Imagine if you had a bookshelf and you put really heavy items on it that it would probably break or collapse. These can be our feelings or thoughts that can make us feel heavy and tired. In order to nurture our vibrations it is good to have a spring clean from time to time.

Polish and clean these shelves and give love to them; be grateful that you have them and that you are creating space for clarity and understanding. You can place any positive thought onto these shelves or whatever comes to your mind. Remember you have these in you already; it is waiting for your love.

Waterfall – This is a very simple technique, because everyone can associate with water when we are washing dishes, clothes, the car, windows or even our children when they are young. Imagine this beautiful place in the middle of a tropical forest where there is this beautiful waterfall with a shallow pond in front of it. Everything is serene, the warm sunrays are peeking through the trees and you can hear the sound of the calm water. See, feel or hear that you are underneath this waterfall and think that it is washing and cleansing your mind, body and soul. Let yourself be one with the love that you are, accept the light in you and acknowledge the strength that you have. You can gently say to yourself: "I love you."

Clarity Box – Sometimes we can feel stuck and experience a lot of negative thoughts, images, sounds or feelings in our mind. We can feel confused and no matter what we do we struggle to find clarity. In order to create clarity, we have to let go of what we are holding on to. An easier way to do this is to create a 'Confusion Box' and place every thought, image, person, sound, and feeling in there, whatever comes up in your mind. Imagine that all these confusing thoughts are locked into your box and when everything you could think of is in there blow it up in your mind or imagine that it has exploded. After this explosion nominate a Clarity Box and place in there what you want or the way you want it to be; in this way you are giving attention to what you do want and will attract more of it.

I wish you an abundance of success with these tools. I would love to hear or read your stories and find out how these techniques worked for you.

Chapter Ten: Closing Words

Thank you for taking the time to read this book. It fills me with joy that I was able to share my experiences with you and that I may in any way have helped you on your journey. Please feel free to share your experience with me; I am always happy to read inspiring stories.

Remember you already have what desire (happiness, confidence, strength, health and wealth) – tap into your soul and see the abundance of love and beauty. I hope that you will hear your heart singing, your soul dancing and your love growing in every moment. You are the artist who can and will transmute your dreams into reality.

I am very grateful for what I already have and have achieved; gratitude empowers me to allow into my life what truly belongs to me.

Good luck on your journey and I wish you, your family, relatives and ancestors love and peace beyond all comprehension.

Andrea

About Andrea

My life has continued to be a colourful journey. I have been through life changing experiences, which were painful at the time, although they contributed to my life.

There were moments, when I felt I was 'struck by lightning'. At some point I found myself at the edge of a platform ready to jump.

My transformation wasn't the easiest, but I am a warrior and from these roller-coaster experiences not only those close to me, but the whole Cosmos continues to benefit.

My purpose in life is to free myself from data with LOVE, because that is when I am truly in the flow.

The solutions are within, whether we are at crossroads, going through health issues, might be experiencing emotional stress or want to reset our life. When we are at zero is when we can experience clarity and invite and allow inspirations into our life.

The people I have worked with in the past were experiencing business problems and wanted to let go of the pressure of expectations; they were harbouring fear or anger within and were not sure how to move forward; some were experiencing panic attacks from money worries or having limiting beliefs about themselves.

I work with people to eliminate these worries and negative thoughts, to release stress and show them how to create freedom and happiness in their life. How to nurture themselves, practice self-care and create a balanced environment.

I am an Alchemist and offer Alchemical sessions online & Advanced Alchemy of the Body treatment face to face to empower, awaken and reset the mind, body & soul. I am also an Alchemical Raw Vegan Food Master / Private Chef and offer consultations and introductions about this type of food online and face to face.

As this chapter of my life closes another one opens and I am sure there will be plenty more adventures to come and experiences to learn from. I am grateful for these golden moments as they were/ are fundamental to my growth.

"Never underestimate your life; it is the greatest gift you have been given."

Andrea Jóba LCH Dip.

www.thefoundationofzero.com
www.rawveganfromtheheart.com